MEGATECH

Internet

Electronic global village

David Jefferis

Crabtree
www.crabtreebooks.com

Introduction

The **Internet** is a computer **network** that makes it possible for people to communicate their thoughts and ideas all over the world. All you need to use the Internet is a desktop computer, a link to an Internet Service Provider (**ISP**), and a screen to display information. Using these tools you can **dial up** and go **surfing** on the Internet's **electronic** sea of information.

In the 1960s, writer Marshall McLuhan predicted that the information age would build an electronic community, where people were linked by ideas rather than by location. McLuhan described this community as a global village, and the Internet provides us with just that.

Crabtree Publishing Company
PMB 16A,
350 Fifth Avenue
Suite 3308
New York
NY 10118

612 Welland Avenue
St. Catharines
Ontario
L2M 5V6

Edited by
Isabella McIntyre
Coordinating editor
Ellen Rodger

Project editors
P.A. Finlay
Carrie Gleason
Production coordinator
Rose Gowsell
Technical consultant
Mat Irvine FRBS
Picture research by
Kay Rowley
Created and produced by
Alpha Communications in association
with Firecrest Books Ltd.

©2002 David Jefferis/Alpha
Communications

Cataloging in Publication Data
Jefferis, David.

Internet : electronic global village/
David Jefferis.
    p. cm.
    Includes index.
    Summary: An introduction to the
history of the Internet and World Wide
Web, how they work, and how they
have changed the way people do
research, buy merchandise, teach,
publish, and communicate.
    ISBN 0-7787-0052-6 -- ISBN 0-
7787-0062-3 (pbk.)
    1. Internet--Juvenile literature. 2.
World Wide Web--Juvenile literature. 3.
Electronic villages (Computer
networks)--Juvenile literature. 4.
Telecommunication--Social aspects--
Juvenile literature. [1. Internet. 2.

World Wide Web. 3.
Telecommunication. 4. Computers and
civilization.] I. Title.
    TK5105.875.I57 J44 2002
    004.67'8--dc21   2001047526
                            LC

Prepress
Embassy Graphics
Printed by
Worzalla Publishing Company

Pictures on these pages, clockwise from far left:
1 Collecting e-mails at breakfast with a laptop computer.
2 Computers still need many cables, wires, and connectors.
3 Digital machines all use a number code based on quantities of "ones" and "zeroes."
4 Most website pages are designed on desktop computers.
5 A World Wide Web electronic postcard site.
6 Viewing a digital camera picture on a computer screen.

Contents

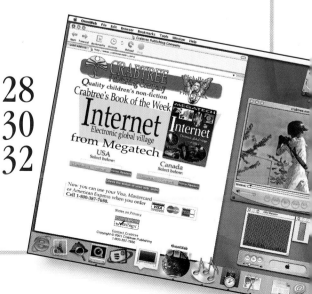

Electronic dawn

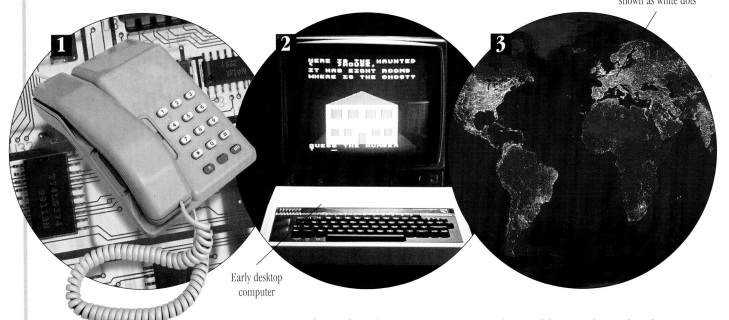

Towns and cities shown as white dots

▲ *Early computers were large machines that were as slow as snails compared to today's computers.*

I t took a combination of three things to make the Internet and **World Wide Web** possible. These things were worldwide telephone links, reliable and fast computers, and **digitization**, or the ability to split words and pictures into tiny **packets** of information.

Early desktop computer

▲ *Telephones (1) and computers (2) were needed for the Internet. Today, there are millions of users, all over the world (3).*

The Internet (or Net) links computers across the world. Joined together by a spider's web of telephone wires, cables, and radio beams, the Internet uses millions of powerful host **server** computers that act as gateways onto the Net. Individual users connect to a host server using desktop **client computers** from work or home. The Internet – it is the sum of millions of parts.

◀ *In the 1960s, the U.S. military worried about communication centers being knocked out in a war. They created ARPAnet, an early form of the Internet.*

G roups of linked computers are called networks, and the Internet is the biggest there has ever been. To use the Net, you connect, or dial up, to a host server computer from your own computer. Once the connection is made, messages are sent around the Net as packets of information by the quickest route.

Host server
computer

Client
computers

▲ *A network is a group of computers that are linked together. Here, a server links a desktop, or client, computer to the Internet through its own link, which is always open.*

▲ *A server is a powerful computer that connects desktop computers to the Internet. A technician adjusts the cables of a server (above). The connections that run behind these machines can seem like a maze of spaghetti even to experts!*

Computers that use the Internet all have their own address code. It is known as an IP (Internet Protocol) address, and works in much the same way as a telephone number. **FTP** (File Transfer Protocol) is another important feature of the Internet. It is software that allows different kinds of computers to communicate and transfer files to any other type of computer linked to the Net.

???

What is digitization?

Digitization is the secret behind today's computing machines, and the key to how the Internet works.

Any information, whether it is numbers, words, pictures, or sounds, can be digitized – changed into the simple machine code that computers use. This is called binary code *because it uses a series of just two numbers, or digits – 1 (one) and 0 (zero).*

Strings of these numbers race around as electronic signals inside a computer. These sets of instructions move at lightning speed, so computers can calculate very quickly. The speed and accuracy of the binary code system allows the Internet to run with millions of computers connected.

The complex computer circuits of this mobile phone can also be used to connect to the Internet

Exploring the Net

▲ *The e-mail system was created in 1972, by an American computer engineer, Ray Tomlinson.*

The Internet's best-known features are electronic mail and the World Wide Web, but there are many other places to visit and use.

Electronic mail (**e-mail**) is an easy way to send a letter using a computer. It is quicker and cheaper than using the post office service, often nicknamed "snail mail." Net users have an e-mail address, where they receive their messages. When an e-mail leaves your computer it goes first to a mail server computer. Then it moves along a chain of mail servers on the Net until it arrives at its destination.

:-)   *Smiling face*

   :-(*Frown or unhappy*

:-D   *Laughing*

   :-/   *A little confused*

0:-)   *Angel face*

   :-x   *My lips are sealed*

:-p   *Sticking tongue out*

   $-)   *Greedy, likes money*

I-O   *Yawning with boredom*

   ;-)   *Happy wink*

◄ *Emoticons or "smileys" first appeared in e-mails in the 1980s. Turn your head sideways to see the expressions. New smileys appear from time to time.*

The mail server system is complex, but it is quick. Speed is the key to the Internet's success, since electronic signals move at lightning speed. For example, an e-mail from Europe to Japan typically takes only a few seconds to arrive.

▲ *Computers store information on a component called the hard disk. This digital memory store is constantly being improved. A computer built in 2001 could store around 1000 times more than one made just ten years earlier.*

What is Netiquette?

Netiquette is the set of unofficial rules that you follow when sending an e-mail or joining a newsgroup discussion.

*   The first rule is to keep your messages short – decide what you are going to say and write it briefly and clearly.*

*   For most e-mails, especially those to strangers, be polite and start as you would a normal letter, with "Dear XXX." And DO NOT TYPE IN CAPITAL LETTERS – in Netspeak, this is like shouting. Politeness is a good general rule – if you annoy someone you may get "flamed" with angry e-mails.*

*   Many people save time by shortening common phrases into code-like acronyms. Examples are FYI – For Your Information, POV – Point Of View, and WRT – With Reference To.*

Another service on the Internet is called Usenet, which is used by newsgroups. Newsgroups are like computer Internet clubs that cover just about every topic you can imagine – sports, hobbies, science, health, business. There are thousands of groups to choose from. Newsgroup members can read, comment, or post new ideas to the group. Their remarks appear in text on screen.

Today you can buy an Internet-linked web camera to show your pictures to the world. In 1991, **webcams** did not exist, and it took coffee-loving researchers at the University of Cambridge, Massachusetts, to come up with the webcam idea. The researchers shared a coffee maker in a hallway outside their offices, and they never knew whether the pot was full or not. They placed a video camera next to the coffee maker and wired the camera to the university's computer network, giving them a perfect view of the pot!

▲ *The Internet reached almost every corner of our planet in the late 1990s. Here Buddhist monks stand outside a Cybercafé in Cambodia. Nearly half of all websites are written in English, making it the first real "world language," understood by billions of people.*

The tiny X-10 webcam can be placed almost anywhere

Coffee cam shows that the pot is empty

▶ *You can travel the world by webcam. Here images are shown from several countries, an ocean liner, two zoos and a wildlife reserve in Africa.*

Viewing the Web

The World Wide Web, or Web, is what really made the Internet popular. The basic unit of display on the Web is an electronic web page. A group of linked pages form a **website**.

▲ *Web pages can be viewed at any time, by any computer that is linked to the Internet.*

The World Wide Web transmits words, pictures, movies, and sounds over the Internet. Using the Web is interesting and easy.

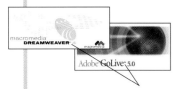

Two popular Web design programs

The World Wide Web is made up of billions of electronic documents called web pages. These pages are linked together electronically to form a website.

In the final website design, this picture will be made smaller, because small images appear quicker on a screen

Netscape Communicator

Microsoft Internet Explorer

▲ *There are many companies that specialize in website design, but beginners can also create sites. All it takes is time, a computer, and a special design* **program.**

▲ *A program called a* **browser** *is used to explore the World Wide Web. A browser allows a computer to display web pages on screen.*

Websites are assembled and designed on a computer, using special web page design software. When a website designer has a website completed, the whole thing is sent to a host computer, where it is stored. The host is linked to the Internet 24 hours a day, and once the site has been stored, anyone on the World Wide Web can look at the information. The great thing about a website is that pages can be added, changed, or removed to update it at any time.

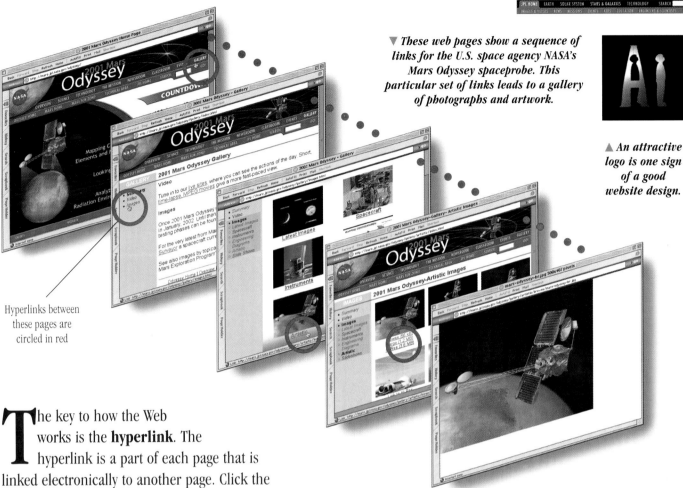

▼ These web pages show a sequence of links for the U.S. space agency NASA's Mars Odyssey spaceprobe. This particular set of links leads to a gallery of photographs and artwork.

▲ An attractive logo is one sign of a good website design.

Hyperlinks between these pages are circled in red

The key to how the Web works is the **hyperlink**. The hyperlink is a part of each page that is linked electronically to another page. Click the hyperlink, and you are taken to another page on the Web. This may be a page on the same site, or it could be a link to related information on another site.

Exploring the Web is known as surfing, but sometimes it seems more like crawling. Just as traffic slows down when a highway becomes very busy, the Web slows down when there is a heavy flow of information or too many surfers are trying to view the same site. Sometimes it is best to try again later!

▼ The variety of website content is as wide as the Web itself. These three sites show a daily cartoon adventure, an author's travels in the United States, and the busy social events of a village in England.

Where did the World Wide Web begin?

The idea of linking pages on an Internet site using hyperlinks belongs to Tim Berners-Lee. He made the proposal in March 1989, while working at the CERN nuclear research laboratory in Switzerland. By Autumn 1990, he had designed the first website and given the project its name, World Wide Web. Soon, scientists started to adopt this easy-to-use system and CERN helped spread the message by publishing computer programming information.

Tim Berners-Lee thought up the name World Wide Web

Google™

YAHOOLIGANS!
the Web Guide for Kids

▲ *There are many search engines. They are all useful, but "Ask Jeeves Kids" and "Yahooligans" are set up especially for younger Web users.*

Speedy information

The Internet is the biggest storehouse of information the world has ever seen, and it grows bigger every day. But how do you find what you want?

With around two billion web pages to choose from, you could click on hyperlinks for a long time before hitting a particular site by chance! The way to find what you want is to search for it. One method is to use a directory service, which has a list of hyperlinks to web pages. The best directories have web pages grouped under various headings. You click through the headings until you start hitting the sites that specialize in the subject you want.

▲ *There are hundreds of online newspapers. They are often electronic versions of paper originals. Many of the same stories are used, but they are presented in a shortened edition for the Web.*

Search engines are similar to directories, but are usually quicker and easier to use. Instead of clicking through headings, you type in key words that sum up your subject. For example, to find a site on the Spanish artist Pablo Picasso, you can simply type in his name. Most search engines sift through the many sites containing the name, and present them as a list, with the most relevant ones at the top. There are over 300 search engines, in many different languages.

◀ *The Sherlock search tool, found on Apple computers, comes with many search engines built in, ready to use.*

For general information, Web editions of newspapers, called e-editions, are great. Most newspapers and magazines have e-editions that you can read without charge. Some magazines offer their best stories on a pay-to-view basis for a week or so, but after that they are also free.

When desktop computers first became popular in the 1980s, many experts predicted that we would not need paper any more, and that offices would be paperless. In fact, the opposite has been the case, and people use more paper now than ever before. Many organizations require that paper records be kept, because electronic equipment changes so fast that a storage medium can be out of date in a few years.

◀ *A hard copy, or printed copy, of a document is often still needed. The latest printers can produce perfect images from Internet files.*

What are URL addresses?

The URL (Uniform Resource Locator) is the address given to a page of information on the Net. Each webpage has its own URL. URLs can be very long, but easy to understand. They need exact copying for a hyperlink to work.

http//www.anyone.co.uk/homepage.html

1   **2**   **3**

1   The "protocol name" shows that it is a web page.
2   The "host name" tells you on what computer and often the country where the page is stored.
3   The "file path" is detailed information that shows exactly where the page is stored in the files and directories of the website.

▶ *Many websites have country code endings, such as the ones shown at right. The code .com is often used by large companies, while .gov is often used by government bodies.*

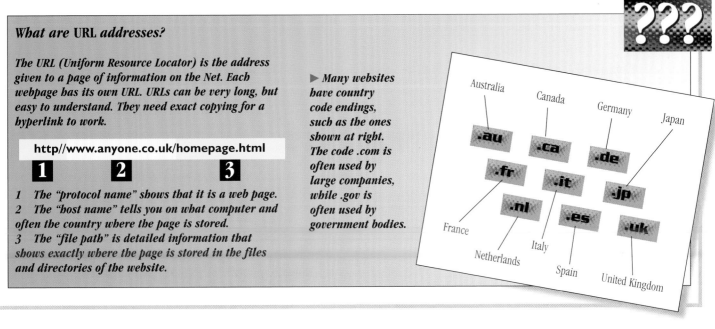

Australia — .au
Canada — .ca
Germany — .de
Japan — .jp
France — .fr
Italy — .it
Netherlands — .nl
Spain — .es
United Kingdom — .uk

Online world

An expert in the 1940s said that the world might need just five computers. In 2001, some families had that many in a single home!

Until the 1990s the Internet was used mostly by people in the military and at universities. When the World Wide Web was introduced, millions of people joined in.

Internet cafés are computer centers that let people send e-mails and use the Web when away from home.

Exact numbers for the World Wide Web are hard to come by. Most figures are best-guesses, as the Web has become so big that no one can keep up. Some figures show that in 1992 about one million computers were linked to the Internet, and there were about 600 websites.

This simplified image of Internet connections gives only a small idea of how complex the Internet is. In reality, there are millions of connecting lines!

Companies that trade on the Web can do so all the time, even at night. It is called 24/7 trading – 24 hours of the day, seven days a week.

Two years later, in 1994, the number of websites had soared past the 10,000 mark. In this year, you could also order a pizza or open an electronic bank account **online** for the first time.

The Web continued to grow. By 1995, there were about 100,000 websites worldwide. Two years later, in Britain, the British Telecom company found that its telephone lines were busier with Internet users than with people talking on the phone. By 2002, there were about two billion pages on the Web, and the numbers are still increasing!

The Internet is also used to exchange commercial information. For example, designers for car companies can swap ideas between offices across the world, quickly and easily.

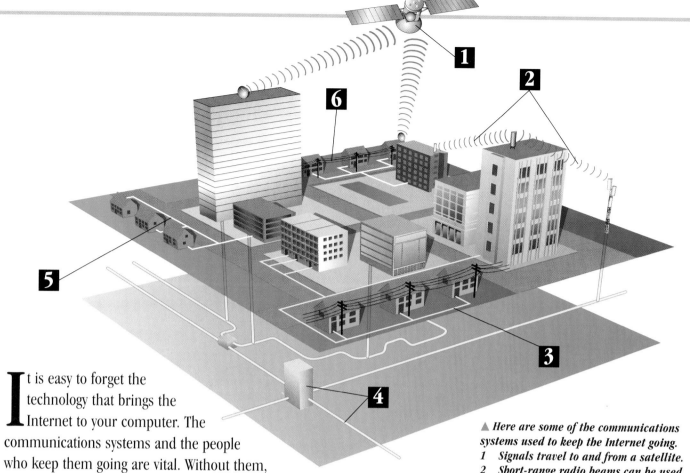

It is easy to forget the technology that brings the Internet to your computer. The communications systems and the people who keep them going are vital. Without them, even the best website would not be seen by anyone!

The networks used for the Internet are a mixture of old and new technologies. Telephones and their lines date back to the nineteenth century, while a satellite link may have been launched by a rocket only a few weeks before. Underground links include **backbones**, which carry large amounts of information between cities, the same way that highways carry traffic.

▲ *Here are some of the communications systems used to keep the Internet going.*
1 Signals travel to and from a satellite.
2 Short-range radio beams can be used between buildings.
3 Optical fiber uses light signals for very fast Internet connections.
4 Long-haul backbone cables link with a regional network through an electronic gateway system.
5 Cable is used for TV and Internet.
6 Telephone lines are used for many home Internet connections.

What are modems *and packets?*

A modem is a handy little gadget that is built into most modern computers. Its function is to link the computer to a server that is linked to the Internet, using a telephone line to make the connection. The equipment in the modem converts information into a form that can travel on ordinary telephone lines. This process is called modulation, hence the name modem, which is short for "modulator-demodulator."

Packets are the way in which information is passed around the Internet. If you send a big computer file, such as a picture, the image is broken down into a number of packets. A lot of small items can travel on the Internet more efficiently than one big one, by taking different routes around the Net as needed. All the packets have the same address details so that they arrive at the right computer. Here they are reassembled to form a single item once again.

A picture of the galaxy is converted into digital packets

Packets travel quickly around the Internet

At their destination, packets are reassembled to form a copy of the original picture

Surfer's paradise

▲ The best websites are attractive and do not take long to appear on screen.

Reading a screen full of useful information is only one part of the Web. Another useful part of the technology is that a computer can copy and store that information for use in the home or office.

Copying a file from the Internet to your computer is called downloading. Some files, especially pictures, can be very large and take a long time to download. It is almost always cheaper and quicker to download information than to have it sent by regular mail. The download speed depends on the connection and type of equipment used.

News sites on the Web tell you what is going on as stories break

Many libraries have websites

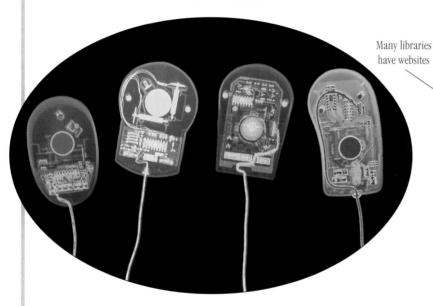

▲ The mouse controls the cursor, or pointing tool, on the computer screen. In this photograph, four computer mice are shown in X-ray form.

There are many programs to download files from the Internet. Freeware programs cost nothing and anyone can use them. Shareware is free at first, but you are expected to pay after a set period, usually 30 days. Trialware is a complete program to try out that stops working after a set period unless you pay for it. Betaware is for testing a new program before it goes on sale.

Students and teachers can get background information to help them with projects

Broadband is a way of speeding up the Internet. When the Net first started, just a few thousand people exchanged mostly text messages. Today, millions of people download big files, so the telephone wires that used to be suitable are now tied up in information traffic jams.

One of the best ways to increase speed is to use optical fiber instead of copper cable. Electric signals are converted into flashes of light, which pass down a very fine plastic tube. One optical fiber can carry at least 1000 times more information than copper cable.

Optical fibers made of fine plastic tubing

Sci-fi movies can be downloaded to a computer's hard disk for viewing on screen

Telephone wires still carry most Internet information

This site lets you send an electronic greeting card

◀ *It would take a lifetime to visit, let alone download, all the sites on the World Wide Web. But the variety means that you are sure to find many sites to match your own interests.*

Computer games and movies are popular on the Internet. An exciting way to play games is online, against other players who may be anywhere in the world. These games can be played between more than two people. Many people play in MUDs, or Multi-User Dungeons, which are usually sci-fi or fantasy adventures. To play online, a computer needs a piece of software called a client. The client enables a machine to communicate with others that are linked to the same online game.

This site tells you about a new type of computer game

▶ *Some online games can be played against other online players. Others can be downloaded and played alone.*

Buying and selling

Most companies have a website to help sell their products. It is possible to live entirely by shopping online, although most people still like to visit a shopping mall from time to time!

▲ *E-commerce is worldwide, using money in many different currencies.*

▲ *Just a few of the many online auction sites.*

Online auctions are big on the Web. Some auction houses, such as eBay and QXL, started off electronically. Others, such as Sothebys, are long-established auction houses that have added e-auctions to their normal business.

In the early days of the World Wide Web, some people thought it would be easy to make a fortune, and there were even those who thought that old-fashioned stores would be killed off by e-business.

It did not work out that way though, and many companies lost money. After all, buying from a website is like mail order, and many people still like to see and feel things before making a purchase. Today, some of the most successful e-businesses are well-known shopping chains that have added websites to their traditional ways of selling.

▲ *Website software shows instant details of customer orders. This lets companies find out quickly how well goods are selling.*

◄ *Some Internet companies set up without calculating the costs properly. One company eventually worked out that it cost it $30 for a truck to deliver each order, no matter how small!*

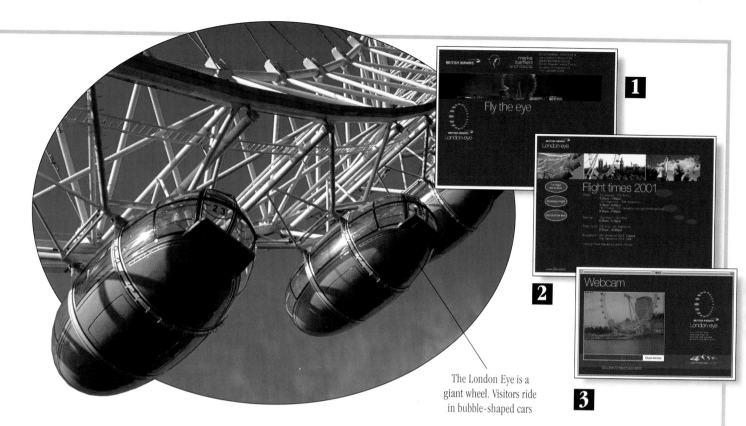

The London Eye is a giant wheel. Visitors ride in bubble-shaped cars

1

2

3

Some things sell well on the Internet. A good example is an airline ticket. If you know where and when you want to go, you can buy a ticket online and not waste time going through a travel agent. Today, many airlines sell most or all of their seats through their websites.

There is still room for a small company with good, original ideas to make it big on the Web, but a familiar name helps because many people feel comfortable dealing with companies they know.

▲ *By 2000, websites had become powerful sales tools. Here, the London Eye ferris-wheel attraction, in Britain, has a website (1) that shows schedules (2), webcam views (3), and an online booking form. There is also a hyperlink to the airline that sponsors the Eye.*

Who buys online?

A lot of people buy online! A 2001 survey showed that over 100 million items had been purchased online by Americans in the previous year. In March 2001 alone, online shoppers spent $3.5 billion!

The Web is changing the way people do business in many ways. People buying houses are likely to visit a website as well as go to a realtor. People buying automobiles haggle harder on price, because they can check the Web for the best deals.

Companies do come out with original sales ideas. In 2001, the Cadbury company sold millions of specially marked candy bars when they ran a contest online. The idea was to find a special code number on a candy bar wrapper, call it in on your mobile phone, and win a prize.

Free soft drink coupon for movie-goers

Countdown timer

▼ *Sites promoting movies are popular on the Web. Movie sites may have free drink coupons, movie posters, even a clock that counts down the time to the movie premiere.*

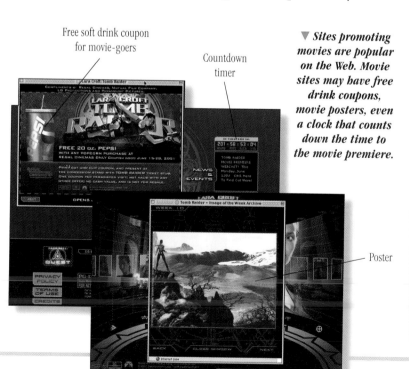

Poster

Convergence

Convergence is the word used for digital machines that can link together. These connections now allow digital machines to share their information.

Digital machines store information on a disk, tape, or **computer chip**. The information is all coded digitally as a stream of "ones" and "zeroes." With the correct program, a computer can read and copy this information, whether it is words, pictures, or music.

▲ *This picture shows a future convergence gadget that can be used as a mobile phone, a diary organizer, for e-mails, and even to view simplified web pages.*

In the late 1990s, websites started to add music as well as images. The sounds were in **MP3** digital format, which made it easy to download them to a computer. Soon the first MP3 players arrived, making it possible to copy your favorite music onto a machine the size of a cassette or CD player. The technology improved to allow you to listen to music in the even better-sounding AAC format, through a wristwatch-sized player!

Napster started as an MP3 music-swap service. By 2000 about 50 million people had used it

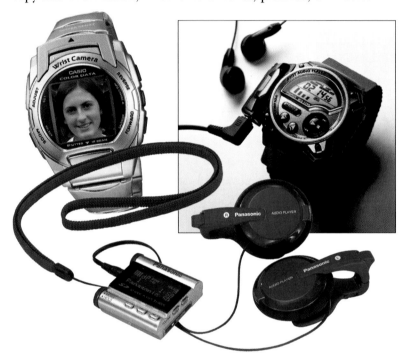

The MP3 format has led to problems. All music is written by someone, and if you buy a CD at a music store, a share of the money goes to the performer, and to the publisher. Free MP3 music meant that musicians and music publishers were not getting paid for their work. The music industry fought back with various plans and formats, such as AAC, which would let them charge for music downloads.

▲ *Internet music players and cameras keep getting smaller. Now you can wear some audio and video products on your wrist.*

◀ *Despite problems with payment rights, there is still no shortage of music on the Internet, and many sites offer MP3 files. Many musicians encourage this by offering free samples of their new songs.*

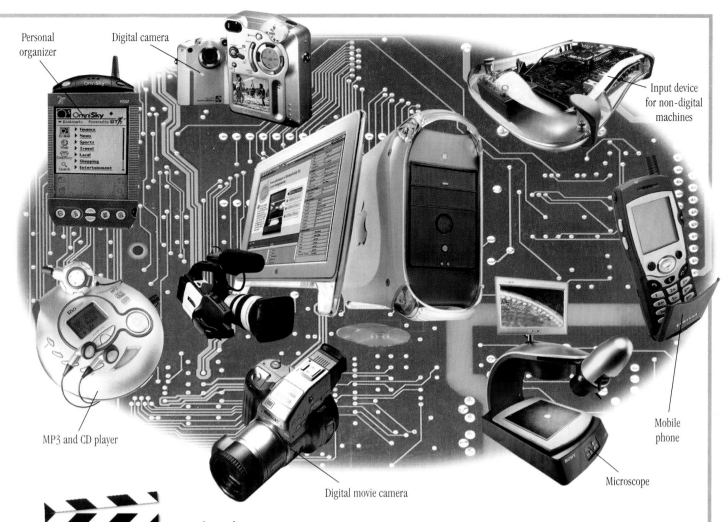

Personal organizer

Digital camera

Input device for non-digital machines

MP3 and CD player

Mobile phone

Microscope

Digital movie camera

▲ *Some of the digital gadgets that can be linked to a computer and the Internet.*

▲ *There are several programs that allow home movie makers to edit their videos. This one is suitable for Apple computers.*

The group of digital machines above are shown converging with a desktop computer at the center. The computer is important because it has the power and speed to process information from these other sources. For example, a **digital camera** can take photos, and even print them using a special adaptor, but you need a computer to store the photos, or to change them easily. Programs are available to make pictures look better and allow you to remove a telephone wire from an otherwise beautiful landscape photograph!

What is a PDA ?

A PDA is a Personal Digital Assistant, an updated version of the old paper organizer. A powerful electronic tool, with functions that range from diary and clock to calculator and notebook, is contained in a diary-sized plastic case. Some of the latest PDAs have plug-in modules. These allow you to go on the Internet, send and receive e-mails, and take small digital pictures. There are PDAs that even have plug-in keyboards if you wish to type in information.

PDAs may soon have electronic paper functions as well. E-paper is a sheet of ordinary-looking paper that is covered with millions of tiny dots. Write on it with a special pen and the patterns of your words or drawings are digitized for downloading to a computer or for e-mailing around the world.

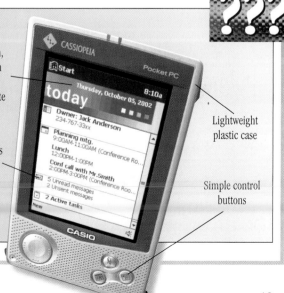

Display screen, here shown in daily planner mode, with date

E-mail zone shows messages received and ready to send

Lightweight plastic case

Simple control buttons

Internet everywhere

▲ *This wristwatch-sized Bluetooth communicator was an early prototype made by the Ericsson mobile-phone maker.*

▲ *Design for a Bluetooth mobile phone.*

Using the Internet once meant sitting at a desk with a computer. New radio technology is changing all that, and soon most things in our homes and offices will be able to communicate without cables or wires.

Some manufacturers already offer wireless systems. Apple computers can use an AirPort Base Station. By plugging the base station into a telephone line, and an AirPort card into the computer, users can surf the Net without needing cables. The base station and computer are linked by radio waves instead of wire. Another wireless solution is **Bluetooth**, which is a local-area system also designed to get rid of the untidy tangle of wires and cables between digital machines.

▲▶ *The Bluetooth computer chip is shorter than a match. A Bluetooth camera (at right) can transmit a picture to a mobile phone, which can then send it as an e-mail.*

The e-fridge from Electrolux was built to include Bluetooth technology. It works on the idea that the kitchen is the most important area of a home. The e-fridge has an Internet screen in the door, which can be used for the Web, e-mail, and ordering food from online suppliers. One day even food packages may have Bluetooth chips, so the e-fridge would know what is inside.

Sensors on future e-fridges may detect rotting food

Door screen can suggest a menu for the day

◀▲ *The e-fridge has a built-in screen on the door for Internet use and for writing electronic post-it notes for the family.*

▲ *The bath and shower area has waterproof controls that check on water temperature, and even monitor when there is enough water in the tub. The toilet uses only a small amount of water so that less water is wasted.*

▲ *The glassed-in area contains a "home portal." This is a communications center that lets family members catch up with useful information on the Web.*

A British mobile phone company opened a special house to test advanced technologies in the early 2000s. They wanted to create an "intelligent house," which would do many things without people in charge. The house has an electronic butler in the form of a software program called Wildfire, which keeps track of many home functions, such as heating and lighting. Wildfire can also place an order with an online grocery store if the kitchen is running low on food. The study area has a webcam for video meetings, and the lawn outside is cut by a robomower. A children's bedroom has a "sound dome," in which you can make as much noise as you like, because it is totally sound-proofed.

▲ *One of the control pads in the house that monitors heat and lights. It also makes sure that curtains are pulled shut at night.*

Will we still need computer keyboards?

People have been forecasting the end of the keyboard for many years, but it is still a useful tool. There are computer programs that can recognize spoken words, and for some things this is very useful. The words "up," "down," "yes," and "no" are simple commands we might use to control a home heating unit. For more complex things, the keyboard is still best. If you want to write a story, for example, you do not want the computer to confuse the words you mutter to yourself with the real ones you want to write! For reasons like this, it is likely that keyboards will be around for many years.

Small keyboard when unfolded

Palm-sized when folded

▲ ▷ *A Design for a small laptop computer, with fold-out keyboard.*

Web warriors

The Internet is a useful electronic tool, but it has its downside too. There are people who use it as an electronic battlefield, to control or destroy distant computer systems.

▲ Anti-virus programs are not new. This one was launched in the late 1980s, and had two upgrades within three years. New viruses appear often, so anti-virus software is updated regularly.

The nastiest way to attack another computer is to introduce a **virus**. Computer viruses are special programs written to confuse or disable the program that allows the machine to operate. Some viruses are harmless, and do no more than make a joke appear on a screen. Others are more serious and can completely wreck a computer. Several companies sell anti-virus programs that are designed to protect computers, but new viruses appear on the Internet from time to time.

▲ The Melissa virus taunted its victims by displaying a Scrabble word used in a cartoon TV series.

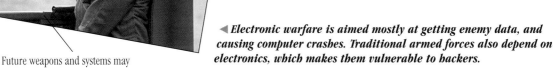

◄ Electronic warfare is aimed mostly at getting enemy data, and causing computer crashes. Traditional armed forces also depend on electronics, which makes them vulnerable to hackers.

Future weapons and systems may communicate with Bluetooth-type chips

Hackers are people who break into other computer systems. Some hackers have full-time jobs in which they are paid to tighten up security systems by showing a system's weaknesses. Others do it for fun.

Crackers are much more serious, and their attacks are a danger to anyone who depends on the Internet. Crackers may break into a system for political reasons or for money.

◄ The "Red Attack" group targeted the computers of the Belgian electricity company Electrabel in 2000. Customers were cut off from the power supply for two hours.

◀ Even public telephones have been hacked. One man made calls by blowing a whistle into the mouthpiece. He did this in such a way that the telephone system was fooled into giving him free long-distance calls!

▶ Even the biggest Internet companies can be sitting ducks for "Quack" attacks. In 2000, Yahoo was jammed by useless information. While the company was sorting it out, crackers snuck in and stole valuable data.

Who is the best-known hacker?

Hackers usually try and keep their identities a secret, but sometimes they get caught. Kevin Mitnick was an expert at hacking his way into computer systems, until he was caught.

The authorities decided to make an example of Mitnick, and he served five years in prison. Upon his release, he was not allowed to use a computer or act as an expert on computer security.

In fact, Mitnick had become the world's most famous hacker. He appeared on many TV and radio shows, as well as giving talks at various computer security conferences. Mitnick's defenders claim he had done little or no actual harm, although no one disputes that he had hacked into computer systems illegally.

▶ *Kevin Mitnick was once on the most-wanted list of the FBI.*

H ackers and crackers are not just people working by themselves. Many countries have secret teams of hackers who back up military forces by waging a war the electronic way. In 2001, the United States and China had an argument over a spy-plane flight, in which a Chinese fighter jet crashed and a U.S. plane made a forced landing on Chinese soil. While the politicians argued, hackers were busy. Chinese hackers attacked several U.S. websites, making pro-China comments appear on them. The hacking was not just one-way. U.S. hackers did similar things to Chinese sites!

Bombing missions can be affected if enemy forces hack into computers that hold target information

▶ *During the Kosovo crisis of 1998-99, Serb e-war forces attacked Allied sites by pinging them. Pinging is normally a simple to-and-fro signal between two computers to check that they can communicate. Pinging can be used for warfare by ordering computers to ping each other until one or more systems crash.*

Big Brother

In 1948 George Orwell wrote a book called *1984*, in which people were constantly watched by the mysterious "Big Brother." Now the Internet makes the idea of such a police state more likely.

In Orwell's story, every citizen had a large television screen, but it was TV with a difference. You could watch it, but it also watched you back. In the novel *1984*, people had no secrets. Today's digital gadgets make it easier to spy on other people than ever before. One example of a spy gadget is the micro-sized webcam. These tiny cameras are cheap and can be placed 100 ft (30 m) away from a computer. Images are sent back by radio link.

▲ *If you make a call from one of the newest mobile phones, your call can be tracked easily and your position checked to within a few hundred yards.*

▼ *This spycam is just one inch (25 mm) long and can send a TV picture 1000 ft (330m) away.*

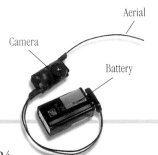

Aerial

Camera

Battery

Companies use personal information when advertising for products. A piece of software called a **web bug** can be used without you knowing. Web bugs can track what you are viewing on your computer, and can then send that information back to a **database** program, which gradually builds up a detailed picture of your habits and interests. This personal information can be sold to companies that design advertisements aimed at your interests. This is not the only way to spy on you. The fictional Big Brother would certainly like to have some of the latest televisions. One design requires the owner to connect to a telephone line when the TV is set up in the home. Every time you switch on, the TV silently keeps tabs on your viewing habits.

▲ *Logging onto the Internet in the morning can trigger distant software programs that track your computer use.*

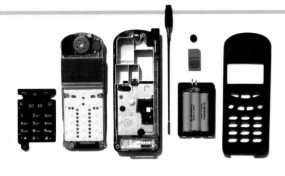

▲ *The same technology that creates tiny mobile phones can also make even tinier spy devices.*

Security cameras are said to reduce crime in city streets and other areas. Software that recognizes human faces is available, and it can be used to spot a person who is wanted by police.

▲ *Computers can scan camera records for wanted faces, using "pattern recognition" software.*

▲ *Websites may collect all sorts of information from people who visit them. Basic details that can be taken easily include the time, date, and length of each visit, and which pages have been seen.*

Do you want to spy on the movements of an automobile? All you need to do is to hide a small spy device on the vehicle, then take it out later. In the meantime, the device records where the vehicle went, its speed, and the distance traveled. Just plug the device into a desktop computer to check it out. A version of this device, which sends out signals as it moves, is used by security services to recover stolen cars. The results are amazing, with almost all stolen vehicles recovered in a few hours.

What is Echelon?

Echelon is a top-secret system that tracks e-mail traffic around the world. Millions of e-mails are tracked every moment, with software that looks for "key words" such as the names of wanted criminals or terrorist organizations.

There are future plans for a data warehouse that would store everyone's e-mails, phone calls, and Internet activity over a period of seven years. The idea is to help police track criminals. One version of this idea is already nicknamed "Big Browser," after the novel 1984. Big Browser could include a detailed record of every website you have ever visited.

What's next?

The Internet is not going to go away. Bluetooth technology could bring it into every part of our lives. In the future, there will be Internet systems in space as well as on Earth.

▲ The Actuality company is planning this globe-shaped 3-D computer screen. Images would no longer be flat, but would look like the real thing, inside the globe.

Not everyone likes the Web. According to a survey in 1999, 10 million U.S. citizens called themselves "former users" of the Internet. But for most of us, the Internet will penetrate every corner of our lives, from surfing with our desktop computers to using convergent machines in our homes.

▶ The latest satellites can broadcast at high speed, so that more Internet traffic can be sent by satellite, rather than along land cables.

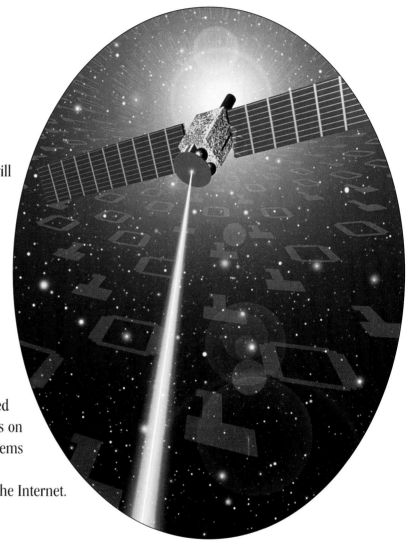

Telematics is the name given to communications devices in vehicles. Some telematic machines will be used for navigation, making sure that a vehicle is on the correct route. Others will check on systems such as the engine and fuel and oil levels. Telematics will also keep us in touch with the Internet.

▼ All but the cheapest future vehicles will have telematic devices. Here are three ideas for future designs.

Mobile phone/Web terminal clips into vehicle steering unit

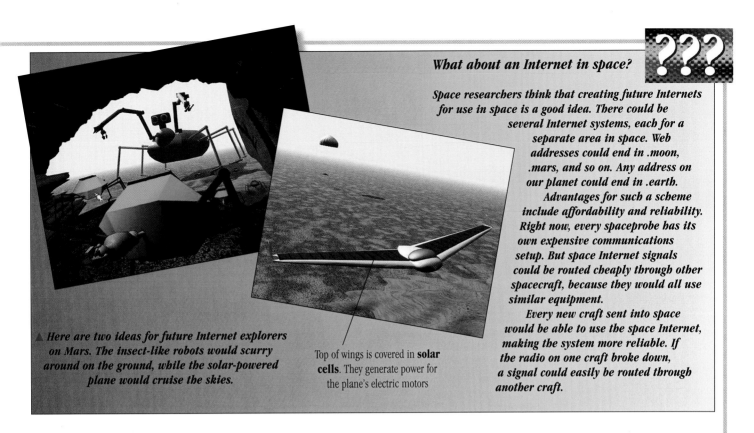

What about an Internet in space?

Space researchers think that creating future Internets for use in space is a good idea. There could be several Internet systems, each for a separate area in space. Web addresses could end in .moon, .mars, and so on. Any address on our planet could end in .earth.

Advantages for such a scheme include affordability and reliability. Right now, every spaceprobe has its own expensive communications setup. But space Internet signals could be routed cheaply through other spacecraft, because they would all use similar equipment.

Every new craft sent into space would be able to use the space Internet, making the system more reliable. If the radio on one craft broke down, a signal could easily be routed through another craft.

▲ *Here are two ideas for future Internet explorers on Mars. The insect-like robots would scurry around on the ground, while the solar-powered plane would cruise the skies.*

Top of wings is covered in **solar cells**. They generate power for the plane's electric motors

I s it a good idea to be in touch constantly? Is it better to go away on vacation or adventures without being interrupted by news from home? For business people, it is important to be available, because if a client cannot reach them, the sale might go to someone else. For people with certain diseases, a constant medical link can be a lifesaver.

For the rest of us, Internet convergence is a mixed blessing. It allows us to be in constant contact with other people, but it means we must be aware that technology can intrude on our privacy.

▼ *In 2001, aircraft makers Boeing and Airbus both decided to launch "Internet in the sky" services. Satellite receivers on airliners will receive popular websites, for display on seat-back video screens for passengers to use.*

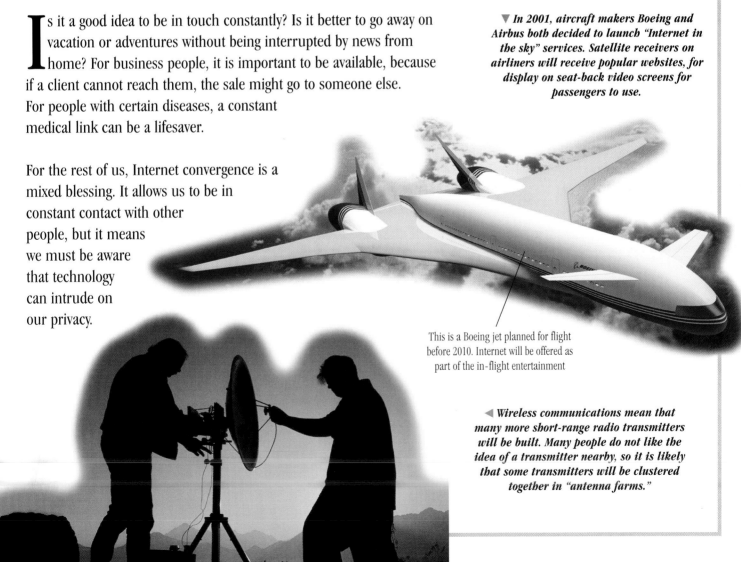

This is a Boeing jet planned for flight before 2010. Internet will be offered as part of the in-flight entertainment

◄ *Wireless communications mean that many more short-range radio transmitters will be built. Many people do not like the idea of a transmitter nearby, so it is likely that some transmitters will be clustered together in "antenna farms."*

Time track

A list of important dates in electronic communications and the Internet, from the work of early pioneers to the present-day and into the future.

▲ *The IC microchip is at the heart of all today's digital machines.*

▲ *In the 1950s, computers were bulky machines. Compared with those of today they were also very slow and unreliable.*

1774 Georges Lesage builds an electric signalling machine called a telegraph. It sends messages between rooms in his home in Geneva, Switzerland.

1850s The telegraph becomes as important in Victorian times as the Internet is today. Messages which used to take weeks between distant countries now take only a few seconds, provided that telegraph lines connect them. But the system sends messages only in **morse code**, not sound or pictures.

1858 The first transatlantic cable is laid for telegraph messages between Europe and the U.S. Today cables connect all continents and are still a main hub of electronic communication.

1876 Alexander Graham Bell makes the first call on his new invention, the telephone. Bell opens a New York to Chicago telephone line in 1892. Telephone lines still provide the main links for the Internet today.

1877 U.S. inventor Thomas Alva Edison makes the first phonograph recording, saying the words: "Mary had a little lamb."

1894 Italian engineer Guglielmo Marconi starts experimenting with radio. He sends messages a distance of about 1.5 miles (2.4 km) in Bologna, Italy.

1901 Marconi sends a radio signal all the way across the Atlantic Ocean, from Britain to Canada, a distance of 2130 miles (3430 km).

1910 Radio helps to catch the murderer Dr. Crippen, who is escaping by sea from Britain to Canada. Unknown to Crippen, the ship's radio officer sends daily messages about him, providing big stories for the world's newspapers.

1921 The first radio station (KDKA of Pittsburgh, U.S.) starts broadcasting.

1926 John Logie Baird from Scotland devises the first working television system. The image is fuzzy, compared to the electronic iconoscope of the Russian-American Vladimir Zworykin.

1937 The first regular TV programs are broadcast, by the BBC. It uses a system based on the iconoscope.

1943 Thomas Watson, chairman of the IBM company, predicts a world market for five computers. He was right in one sense – early computers were huge and few people would have had room to store them. For example, the IBM UNIVAC I was as big as a one-car garage.

1945 British writer Arthur C. Clarke suggests using satellites to send radio and TV signals around the world. Clarke later becomes famous for writing many science-fiction stories.

1945 U.S. computer pioneer Vannevar Bush says that the future will be an age of information. His ideas include the memex, a "storehouse of knowledge," and the Cyclops camera to be worn on the forehead. In Bush's words, the Cyclops could, "photograph anything you see and want to record," much like a palm-size video camera of today.

◄ *This Arthur C. Clarke book has many fascinating ideas about electronic communications in the future.*

1946 U.S. team builds the first digital computer, ENIAC. All today's desktop computers are digital machines.

1948 The transistor is developed by U.S. researchers John Bardeen, Walter Brattain and William Shockley. It allows electronic devices to be smaller, cheaper, and much more reliable.

1953 The color TV system is adopted by the U.S. for broadcasting.

1956 The first video recorder is developed by an Ampex Corporation research team in the U.S.

1956 The first transatlantic telephone line is laid, allowing up to 36 telephone conversations at a time.

1957 Russia launches the first artificial satellite, Sputnik 1. Today, satellites are vital for communications, including most Internet traffic.

1958 U.S. engineer Jack Kilby assembles the first integrated circuit (IC). On this, electronic components are put together in one tiny assembly called a microchip.

1960 U.S. programmer Ted Nelson writes the hypertext computer language. This makes possible a "hotlinked" trail of related electronic information sites, and is the basis of today's World Wide Web.

1962 The first communications satellite (**comsat**) is launched. Telstar is basketball-sized, and relays TV across the Atlantic Ocean. Today, there are hundreds of comsats in space.

1962-1968 Packet-switching technology is developed. The Internet uses this system, which reduces information to tiny pieces, or packets.

▲ This wristwatch-sized digital machine is designed for playing music from Internet MP3 files.

▲ The Watchphone was introduced in 2000. For the first time a mobile phone was small enough to wear on the wrist.

1969   U.S. Defense Department's ARPAnet network is started. The idea is to build an attack-proof communications system for the military.

1970s   Electronic devices using IC microchips become available.

1971   The first microcomputers become available. They are used mostly by large corporations and governments.

1972   American Ray Tomlinson creates electronic mail (e-mail).

1972   ARPAnet is demonstrated with 40 machines linked together. It is connected to organizations in Britain and Norway, the first international linkup.

1974   Telnet is opened, a commercial version of ARPAnet.

1975   The first desktop Personal Computer (PC) is developed by IBM.

1979   First newsgroups go online on a part of the Internet called Usenet.

1980s   Personal computers start to be used widely in offices.

1980s   Universities and corporations develop LANs (Local Area Networks) for their computers, many linked to other networks. By the late 1980s, people are using these systems regularly for e-mails.

1984   Apple Macintosh computer uses a GUI (Graphical User Interface), which makes computers easier to use. The later Windows system looks similar.

1984   DNS (Domain Name Server) system used for computer addresses made of easy-to-remember words, rather than a long number.

1984-87   Number of host computers increases from 1000 to more than 28,000.

1989   The launch of the World Wide Web, a system that allows Internet users to have graphics and sound, as well as text.

1990   Host computers pass 300,000 and there are over 1000 newsgroups.

1990s   Personal computers start to be used in large numbers by people in homes as well as offices.

1991   WAIS (Wide Area Information Server) is developed to create an index of the Internet's contents.

1991   CERN releases World Wide Web program information. A version which can show graphics follows two years later.

1992   There are now more than a million host computers on the Internet.

1993   The World Wide Web starts to grow quickly. According to one study, in June 1993 there were just 130 websites. Three months later there were 204, and by Christmas there were 623.

1993   The U.S. White House and the United Nations go online.

1994   The number of people using the Internet passes 25 million. There are 10,000 websites and the first shopping sites (pizza and banking) go online.

▶ Large ground stations are used to exchange electronic information with satellites passing overhead in space.

1996   There are now over 500,000 websites online, and more than 12 million host computers.

1998   The number of e-mails sent worldwide nears three trillion a year.

2000   Steve Jobs of Apple Computer says that digital machines are converging on the digital hub that is the home computer.

2001   Five U.S. airlines join together to sell tickets online. European and other airlines plan similar schemes.

2001   Aircraft makers Boeing and Airbus announce plans to fit Internet screens in passenger cabins.

The future
Remote-operated rover vehicle sent to the Moon. For a fee, people can drive it, using game-style controls on the website.

Most people have high-speed Internet connections that can transmit the contents of a multi-volume encyclopedia in one second.

The world relies on the Internet and World Wide Web for most information and trade.

Wristwatch-size webphones allow communications anywhere on Earth.

Internets developed for bases on the Moon, Mars, and other space habitats.

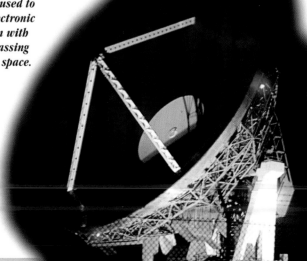

Glossary

▲ *Pictures from a digital camera can be saved on a computer for storage or for printing later.*

A n explanation of the technical terms and concepts used in this book.

▲ *Bluetooth equipment ranges from mobile phones to refrigerators.*

ARPAnet
U.S. Defense Department computer network of the 1960s, the forerunner of today's Internet. The name comes from Advanced Research Project Agency.

Backbone
A main carrier of heavy Internet traffic.

Binary code
Computer code system that uses arrangements of ones and zeroes.

Bluetooth
Technology that allows machines to communicate together with radio signals.

Browser
A program that acts as a "window" to the World Wide Web. A browser lets users go to a search engine or to websites. The most popular browsers are Microsoft Internet Explorer and Netscape Communicator.

▼ *A closeup of the circuits and components in a fairly simple piece of hardware, the mouse.*

CERN
The European international research center for nuclear research, based outside Geneva, Switzerland. It is where the World Wide Web started, to share research files.

Client computer
Computer used to connect to a host computer, which in turn links the client to the Net.

Communications satellite (comsat)
Spacecraft in near-Earth orbit that relays radio and TV signals around the planet. A system of nearly 300 satellites is planned in the future as an "Internet in the Sky" for users of all digital equipment, from telephones to computers.

Computer chip
Electronic circuit that has all parts needed for operation (apart from knobs, buttons, and screen) on a tiny chip of silicon. Also known as a "microchip" for its small size. Used in almost all electronic gadgets.

Convergence
Word which means "coming together." In computing and Internet, it means all digital machines being able to exchange information through a desktop computer that becomes the digital "hub."

Cracker
See Hacker.

Cybercafé
Place that people can visit to surf the Internet. Computers are hired by the time spent online.

Database
A program that can record and show lists of facts and figures. Examples of databases include lists of names, addresses, phone numbers, viewing habits, and so on.

Dial up
Connecting to the Internet. Making the connection is called logging on.

Digital, digitized
A piece of equipment that uses the one-and-zero computer system, in which all information is reduced to a stream of electronic signals. Using a video camera or other piece of equipment, words, pictures, and sounds can be "digitized," or converted to a digital form.

Digital camera
Camera that uses a light-sensitive computer chip, rather than film.

Electronic
Describes any equipment that works by adjusting the flow of electrons moving through a circuit, from radios and tape players to computers and televisions.

E-mail
Electronic mail, a system of sending and receiving messages through the Internet. Users who like the speed and ease of e-mail usually refer to post office service as "snail mail."

Emoticon
Typing in a symbol to show an emotion when you type an e-mail. It is also known as a smiley :)

FTP
File Transfer Protocol, the software that allows different types of computers to use the Internet.

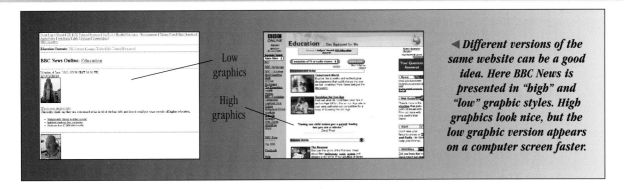

Different versions of the same website can be a good idea. Here BBC News is presented in "high" and "low" graphic styles. High graphics look nice, but the low graphic version appears on a computer screen faster.

Hacker
Amateur who likes to break ("hack") into other people's computer systems. Hackers are sometimes harmless, unlike crackers, who are professional criminals intent on stealing information or wrecking a system.

Home page
The first page presented when you visit a website. It acts in the same way as the contents page of a book.

Hyperlink
See Hypertext.

Hypertext
Computer program that allows a user to view a site on the World Wide Web. To go to another web page, you click on a part of your screen called a hyperlink, or hotlink.

Internet
Global network linking millions of computers able to exchange information.

ISP
Internet Service Provider. A company that individual Internet users pay to link them to the Internet. The ISP also acts as a "post office" for e-mail.

Modem
Device that connects a computer to the Internet using a telephone line. It converts computer code into a form that can travel on ordinary telephone lines.

Morse code
Dot-dash signal code devised by Samuel Morse in 1838. The letter "a" is represented as dot-dash; "b" as dash-dot-dot-dot, and so on for all the alphabet and numbers 1 to 10. Morse code is a simple digital system, but is far slower than the electronic code used in computing.

MP3
A computer file format for digital music, usually available for download from music sites on the World Wide Web.

Network
A group of computers that are linked, allowing users to share information. Intranets are self-contained networks, often used by big companies. A LAN is a Local Area Network.

Online
Being connected to the Internet.

Optical fiber
Ultra-fine plastic tube through which light can pass. Computers can use optical fibers with equipment that changes electronic code to light signals. The big advantage of using optical fiber is that it can carry at least 10,000 times as much information as telephone wire.

Packet
Small piece of a larger amount of computer information.

PDA
Personal Digital Assistant, a hand-held electronic organizer.

Ping
Signal sent between two computers to check communications between them.

Program
A set of instructions that makes a computer work in a particular way. A program may be for calculating, word processing, for graphics, or for thousands of other uses. Computer programs are generally lumped together in the catch-all word, software. The equipment needed to run software is called hardware.

Search engine
World Wide Web software that allows a user to search the Web for information. It works like an electronic telephone book.

Server
Also known as a host, the type of computer used by an ISP to link users with the Internet and World Wide Web.

Solar cells
Flat panels that can convert the energy in light to electricity. They are used in many machines, from pocket calculators to giant satellites the size of a truck.

Surfing
A term first used in 1992 to describe going from site to site on the World Wide Web.

Telematics
Technology that puts Internet-type machines into moving vehicles, such as automobiles.

URL
Uniform Resource Locator. Name for a World Wide Web address.

Virus
Software program that attacks programs on other computers. Like a virus in a living organism, it can copy itself and spread, hence the name. Viruses can be transmitted on the Internet, on memory disks, e-mails, even CD-ROMs. The only answer is a virus detection program, which is designed to search and destroy viruses.

Web bug
Software that can track and record information about a website visitor.

Webcam
Video camera that can show images through a computer on to the Internet.

Website
Method of presenting information on the World Wide Web, with a home page showing the site's contents. Clicking on hypertext hotlinks takes a user away from the home page, to other electronic pages on the website. Sites also often have links to other sites that have additional or related information.

World Wide Web (WWW)
Part of the Internet that is designed as indexed and linked graphic pages.

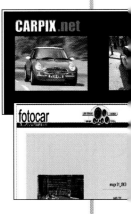

▲ *Cars and car racing are popular on the Web. Here, two photographers have created their own websites to sell their photos.*

Index

Acknowledgements
We wish to thank all those individuals and organizations that have helped create this publication.

Photographs were supplied by:
Alpha Archive
Tim Andrew
Apple Computer
BBC
Boeing Corp
British Airways
Cadbury Confectionery
Casio Corp
CNN News
Direct Tek
Duality Corp
Electrolux
Ericsson
HST Hubble Space telescope
Mat Irvine
Isuzu Cars
David Jefferis
Lockheed Martin Corp
Marco Lukovic (car design for Peugeot)
Microsoft Corp
NASA
Netscape Corp
Nokia
Northrop Grumman Corp
Orange SA
Panasonic Corp
Peugeot Cars
Science Photo Library
Sony Corp

Digital art created by:
Gavin Page